LET THE ADVENTURES BEGIN!

We're so glad you've decided to explore the National Parks with us! This book will help you navigate your way through all the parks in the Western Region.

This region is made up of islands and a wide range of landforms and climates in the Western United States.

During your visit to the Park be sure to meet one of the Park Rangers and get your book stamped!

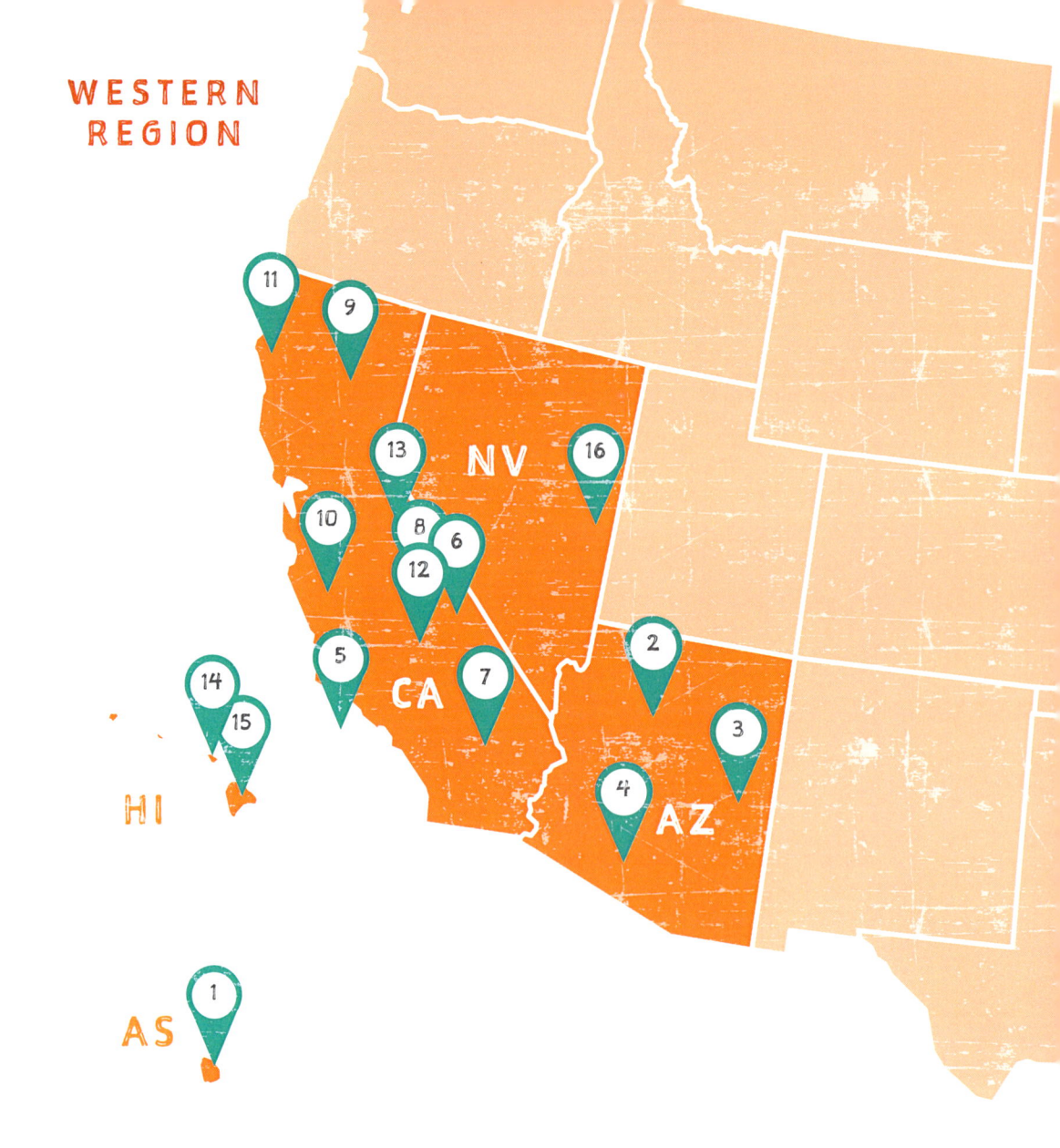

WESTERN REGION

NV
CA
AZ
HI
AS

2

WESTERN REGION
Table of Contents

AMERICAN SAMOA
1. American Samoa, AS 4

ARIZONA
2. Grand Canyon, AZ 8
3. Petrified Forest, AZ 12
4. Saguaro, AZ 16

CALIFORNIA
5. Channel Islands, CA 20
6. Death Valley, CA 24
7. Joshua Tree, CA 28
8. Kings Canyon, CA 32
9. Lassen Volcanic, CA 36
10. Pinnacles, CA 40
11. Redwood, CA 44
12. Sequoia, CA 48
13. Yosemite, CA 52

HAWAII
14. Haleakala, HI 56
15. Hawai'i Volcanoes, HI 60

NEVADA
16. Great Basin, NV 64

"I stood and looked. Everything was peaceful, and it rested me."
—Minerva Hamilton Hoyt

AMERICAN SAMOA NATIONAL PARK
American Samoa

51st National Park

Established in **1993**

13,500 acre park
9,500 land & 4,000 marine acres

21 square miles

3 Islands
TA'U, OFU, AND TUTUILA

AS

AMERICAN SAMOA NATIONAL PARK
Record Your Visit

Date: _____

This is the ___ park I've visited. We were in the park for _____ .
      #   hours/days

The weather was _____ .

My favorite memory of our visit was _____ .

I met Park Ranger _____ who has been here for _____ .
                                                                                               months/years

Their favorite part of the park is _____

_____ .

Park Ranger autograph:_____

Cancellation & Regional Stamp(s)

AMERICAN SAMOA NATIONAL PARK
What to Look For

- As the Pacific Ocean plate moved across a stationary hot spot, a **LINE OF VOLCANOES** formed above the water's surface, three of which make up the American Samoa National Park.

- **FRUIT BATS** are active both day and night. Their wing span can reach up to 3 feet. That's almost the same as a baseball bat.

- More than **800 NATIVE FISH AND 200 CORAL SPECIES** are bewildering and beautiful.

- **HUMPBACK WHALES** grow up to 50 feet and weigh about 45 tons. That's like three school buses!

- Plant communities of the park are largely **TROPICAL RAINFORESTS**.

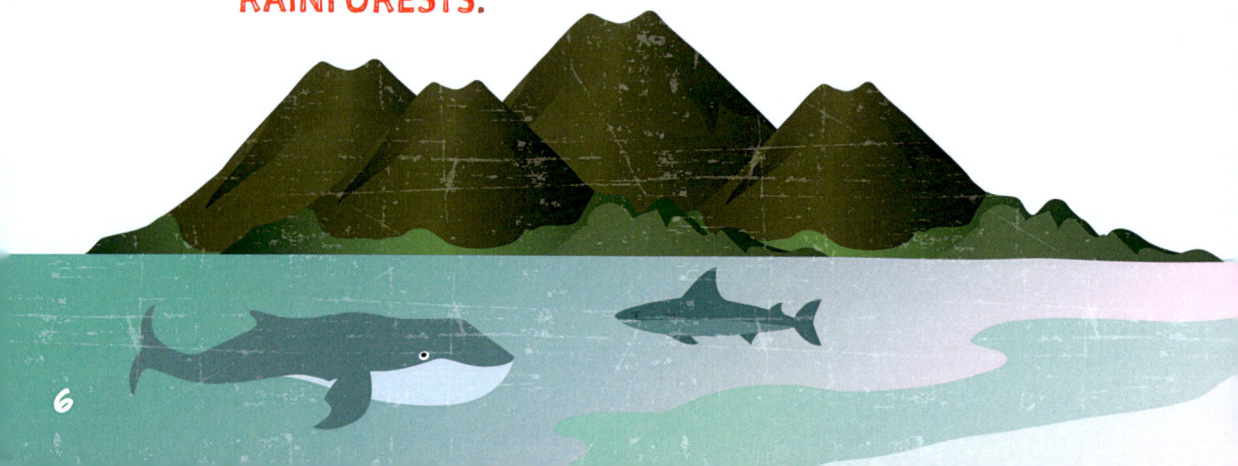

AMERICAN SAMOA NATIONAL PARK
Interesting Facts

- The National Park of American Samoa is in the **HEART OF THE SOUTH PACIFIC.**

- The park is the only American National Park **SOUTH OF THE EQUATOR.**

- **TALOFA** means **HELLO** in Samoan.

- **SAMOA** means **"SACRED EARTH."** The park protects the 3,000 year old Samoan culture.

GRAND CANYON NATIONAL PARK
Arizona

13th National Park

1,201,647 acre park

Established in **1919**

Deepest Point is at **6,000 ft**

1,878 square miles

AZ

GRAND CANYON NATIONAL PARK
Record Your Visit

Date: _____

This is the ____ park I've visited. We were in the park for _____ .
        #   hours/days

The weather was _____ .

My favorite memory of our visit was _____ .

I met Park Ranger _____ who has been here for _____ .
                                                                                                               months/years

Their favorite part of the park is _____

_____ .

Park Ranger autograph:_____

Cancellation & Regional Stamp(s)

GRAND CANYON NATIONAL PARK
What to Look For

- The **KAIBAB LIMESTONE** is the uppermost layer of rock at the Grand Canyon.

- One of the rarest and largest birds in the world, the **CALIFORNIA CONDOR**, can be found at the Grand Canyon.

- **GILA MONSTERS** are large, thick-bodied lizards identified by their distinct black and orange coloration.

- Cacti are plentiful at the Grand Canyon. Try to spot the **FISHHOOK CACTUS** by its beautiful pink and purple flowers.

GRAND CANYON NATIONAL PARK
Interesting Facts

- The **GRAND CANYON** has been developing for over 5 million years as the Colorado River carves through it.

- Geologists call the process of canyon formation **DOWNCUTTING** which is long term vertical erosion.

- The **SOUTH RIM** has the most visitors, whereas the **NORTH RIM** is more secluded.

- **ARCHEOLOGISTS** have made many discoveries of ancient peoples who lived in the area.

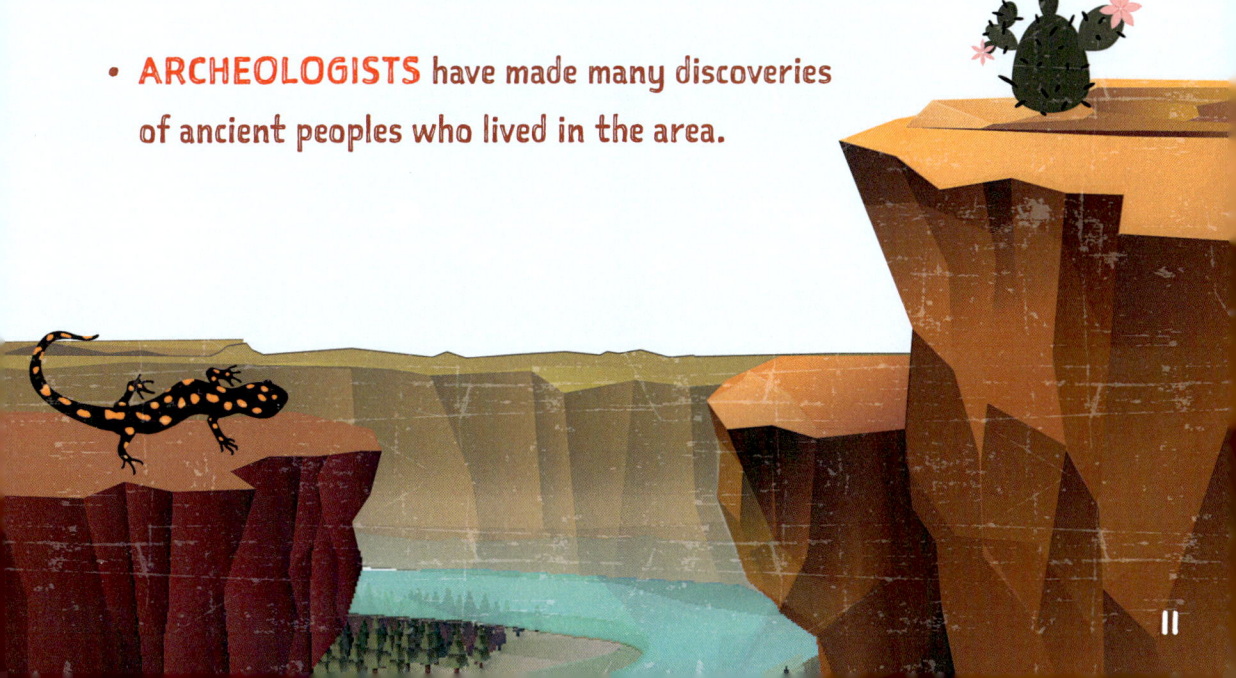

PETRIFIED FOREST NATIONAL PARK
Arizona

30th National Park

Established in **1962**

Located in the **Greater Painted Desert**

346 square miles

221,390 acre park

AZ

PETRIFIED FOREST NATIONAL PARK
Record Your Visit

Date: _____

This is the ____ park I've visited. We were in the park for _____ .
        #   hours/days

The weather was _____ .

My favorite memory of our visit was _____ .

I met Park Ranger _____ who has been here for _____ .
                                                                                                       months/years

Their favorite part of the park is _____

_____ .

Park Ranger autograph: _____

Cancellation & Regional Stamp(s)

PETRIFIED FOREST NATIONAL PARK
What to Look For

- The **JUNIPER** has scale-covered leaves and bluish, waxy-coated seeds that help the tree conserve moisture.

- The unique **AMERICAN AVOCET**, a long-legged wading bird, has a distinct upturned bill.

- Mounds of fresh soil indicate a **BOTTA POCKET GOPHER** is near.

- While hiking, try to find the beautiful **CRYPTANTHAS** characterized by its popcorn-like flower buds.

PETRIFIED FOREST NATIONAL PARK
Interesting Facts

- The Petrified Forest is known for its fossils, especially its **FALLEN TREES** that thrived more than 225 million years ago.

- Ancient peoples built **AGATE HOUSES** using petrified wood as a building material.

- Spanish explorers named the region **EL DESIERTO PINTADO**— The Painted Desert.

- Between 1857 and 1860 the US Government conducted an experiment using **CAMELS AS DESERT TRANSPORT.**

SAGUARO NATIONAL PARK
Arizona

52nd National Park

Established in **1994**

143 square miles

Home to Nation's **Largest Cacti**

91,716 acre park

AZ
4

SAGUARO NATIONAL PARK
Record Your Visit

Date: _____

This is the ____ park I've visited. We were in the park for _____ .
      #   hours/days

The weather was _____ .

My favorite memory of our visit was _____ .

I met Park Ranger _____ who has been here for _____ .
                                                                                                                         months/years

Their favorite part of the park is _____

_____ .

Park Ranger autograph: _____

Cancellation & Regional Stamp(s)

SAGUARO NATIONAL PARK
What to Look For

- The **IRONWOOD**, covered with lilac-colored blossoms, is one of the Sonoran Desert's most beautiful trees.

- **JAVELINAS** are known for eating prickly pear cactus. Despite their appearance, they are not in the pig family.

- **GILA WOODPECKERS** are architects of the Sonoran Desert by carving homes in saguaros throughout the park.

SAGUARO NATIONAL PARK
Interesting Facts

- **PRESIDENT HERBERT HOOVER** named Saguaro a **NATIONAL MONUMENT** shortly before he left office in 1933.

- **CACTUS FOREST DRIVE** is an 8.4 mile scenic loop that has been placed on the National Register of Historic Places.

- **SAGUARO CACTUS** survive an average of 125 years and weigh up to 6 tons and can grow as tall as 50 feet.

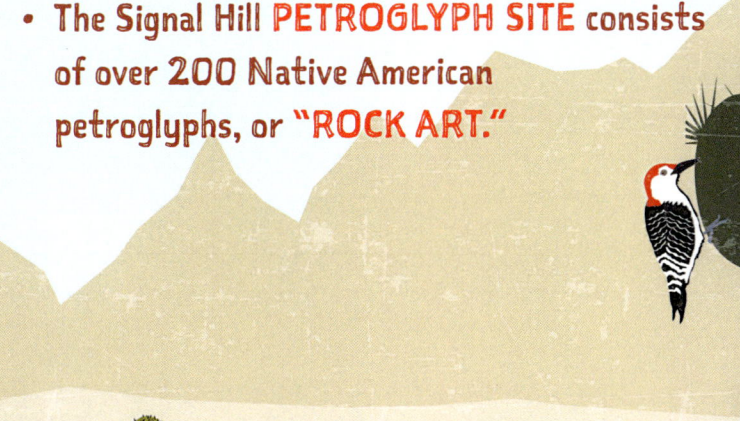

- The Signal Hill **PETROGLYPH SITE** consists of over 200 Native American petroglyphs, or **"ROCK ART."**

CHANNEL ISLANDS NATIONAL PARK
California

249,561 acre park

40th National Park

390 square miles

Established in **1980**

Five Remarkable Islands off the coast of Southern California

CHANNEL ISLANDS NATIONAL PARK
Record Your Visit

Date: _____

This is the ____ park I've visited. We were in the park for _____ .
      #   hours/days

The weather was _____ .

My favorite memory of our visit was _____ .

I met Park Ranger _____ who has been here for _____ .
                                                                                                                     months/years

Their favorite part of the park is _____

_____ .

Park Ranger autograph:_____

Cancellation & Regional Stamp(s)

CHANNEL ISLANDS NATIONAL PARK
What to Look For

- **DOLPHINS** are spotted riding the bow waves on boat rides over to the islands.

- The most familiar marine mammal to the Channel Islands is the **CALIFORNIA SEA LION.** They are named after lions because of their loud roars and barking.

- Present on every island is the **COASTAL SAGE SCRUB**, an important habitat for a variety of animals.

- Brilliant **YELLOW COREOPSIS** on Santa Barbara Island usually show their brightest colors between late January and March.

CHANNEL ISLANDS NATIONAL PARK
Interesting Facts

- The **ANACAPA ISLAND** lighthouse was the last permanent lighthouse built on the West Coast.

- Painted Cave on **SANTA CRUZ ISLAND** is one of the largest known sea caves in the world.

- **SAN MIGUEL ISLAND** has one of the largest congregations of wildlife in the world.

- Experienced kayakers can circumnavigate **SANTA BARBARA'S** five mile coastline.

- Great tidepooling spots are located in Bechers Bay on **SANTA ROSA ISLAND**.

DEATH VALLEY NATIONAL PARK
California

3,373,063 acre park

53rd National Park

Established in **1994**

5,270 square miles

Hottest, Driest, Lowest
National Park

DEATH VALLEY NATIONAL PARK
Record Your Visit

Date: _____

This is the ____ park I've visited. We were in the park for _____ .
        #   hours/days

The weather was _____ .

My favorite memory of our visit was _____ .

I met Park Ranger _____ who has been here for _____ .
                                                                                                                months/years

Their favorite part of the park is _____

_____ .

Park Ranger autograph: _____

Cancellation & Regional Stamp(s)

DEATH VALLEY NATIONAL PARK
What to Look For

- The **DESERT TORTOISE** is able to live in exceedingly hot temperatures by digging underground burrows to escape the heat.

- An abundant butterfly species is the **WESTERN PYGMY BLUE**.

- If there is plentiful rain in the winter **DESERT WILDFLOWERS** can be spectacular in the spring.

- **BURROS (OR DONKEYS),** have colors ranging from black, white, brown, and gray or they can be striped, spotted or speckled.

DEATH VALLEY NATIONAL PARK
Interesting Facts

- **TIMBISHA SHOSHONE INDIANS** lived in the area for centuries.

- Death Valley is the **LARGEST** National Park in the lower 48 states.

- Death Valley got its name from a fateful trip taken by pioneers in the 1840's when they proclaimed **"GOODBYE DEATH VALLEY."**

- Death Valley mining companies had **20 MULE TEAMS** that pulled almost 40 tons of borax (soap) over 165 miles in 10 days. Amazing!

JOSHUA TREE NATIONAL PARK
California

790,636 acre park

54th National Park

Established in **1994**

1,236 square miles

CA

7

lifespan of a Joshua Tree averages **150 years**

28

JOSHUA TREE NATIONAL PARK
Record Your Visit

Date: _____

This is the ____ park I've visited. We were in the park for _____ .
         #   hours/days

The weather was _____ .

My favorite memory of our visit was _____ .

I met Park Ranger _____ who has been here for _____ .
                                                                                                          months/years

Their favorite part of the park is _____

_____ .

Park Ranger autograph: _____

Cancellation & Regional Stamp(s)

JOSHUA TREE NATIONAL PARK
What to Look For

- The **ROADRUNNER** can clock up to 20 mph!

- Rodents, like the **DUSKY CHIPMUNK**, can hide in rocky crevices to avoid the heat.

- The **JOSHUA TREE** provides food and shelter for many birds, mammals, reptiles, and insects.

- The **CHOLLA CACTUS GARDEN** is a must see spot.

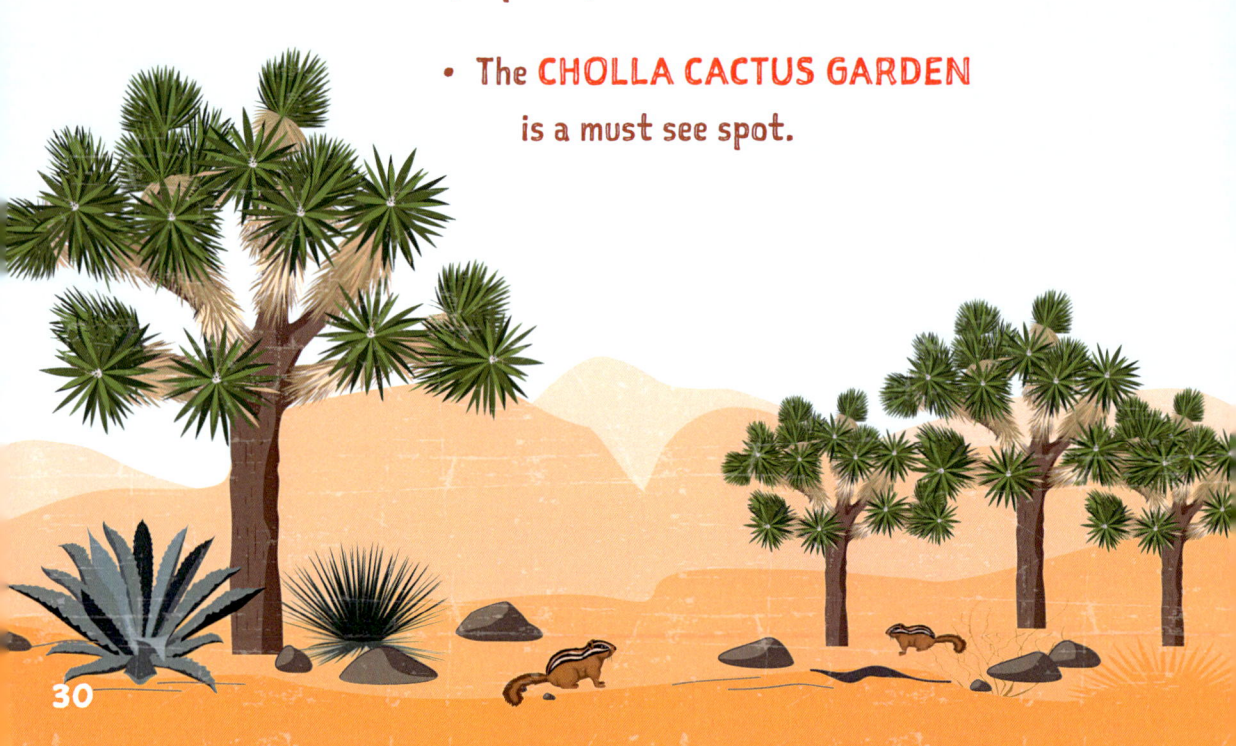

JOSHUA TREE NATIONAL PARK
Interesting Facts

- The **OASIS OF MARA** was settled by the Serrano who called it "the place of little springs and much grass."

- **MINERVA HOYT** founded the National Deserts Conservation League and **ELIZABETH CAMPBELL** was a pioneer in desert archaeology.

- **BARKER DAM** is on the National Register of Historic Places.

KINGS CANYON NATIONAL PARK
California

461,901 acre park

22nd National Park

Established in **1940**

722 square miles

CA 8

General Grant Sequoia
is the 2nd largest living tree

KINGS CANYON NATIONAL PARK
Record Your Visit

Date: _____

This is the ____ park I've visited. We were in the park for _____ .
        #   hours/days

The weather was _____ .

My favorite memory of our visit was _____ .

I met Park Ranger _____ who has been here for _____ .
                                                                                        months/years

Their favorite part of the park is _____

_____ .

Park Ranger autograph: _____

Cancellation & Regional Stamp(s)

KINGS CANYON NATIONAL PARK
What to Look For

- **WESTERN POND TURTLES** can be found basking on logs or boulders. These turtles are small, only growing 8 inches in length.

- Recognized by its plume, 6 feathers that droop forward on the head, is the **CALIFORNIA QUAIL**.

- The small area of the wetlands provide important habitat for **FLAME SKIMMERS** that need standing water to lay their eggs.

KINGS CANYON NATIONAL PARK
Interesting Facts

- The **CEDAR GROVE** area offers several trails.

- The **GIANT SEQUOIA** sprouts from seeds and can live over **3,000 YEARS**.

- A major factor in the longevity of giant sequoias is a chemical called **TANNIN**, which is present in sequoia bark. Tannin gives the sequoia resistance to rot, boring insects and fire.

LASSEN VOLCANIC NATIONAL PARK
California

106,589 acre park

10th National Park

Established in **1916**

166 square miles

Lassen Peak is an active volcano

LASSEN VOLCANIC NATIONAL PARK
Record Your Visit

Date: _____

This is the ___ park I've visited. We were in the park for _____ .
     #   hours/days

The weather was _____ .

My favorite memory of our visit was _____ .

I met Park Ranger _____ who has been here for _____ .
                                                                                                                      months/years

Their favorite part of the park is _____

_____ .

Park Ranger autograph: _____

Cancellation & Regional Stamp(s)

LASSEN VOLCANIC NATIONAL PARK
What to Look For

- The **SIERRA NEVADA RED FOX**, a threatened species, may be spotted hunting for food.

- Recognized by its distinctive, single white patch on its cheek is the **BUFFLEHEAD DUCK**.

- **MULE'S EARS**, sunflower-like flowers, bloom beneath Mount Diller.

LASSEN VOLCANIC NATIONAL PARK
Interesting Facts

- All four types of volcanoes found in the world are in Lassen: **SHIELD, COMPOSITE, CINDER CONE AND PLUG DOME.**

- The **US GEOLOGICAL SOCIETY'S** first volcano observatory was developed at Lassen Volcanic Center in the early 20th century.

- Lassen is considered to be a **"HIGH THREAT" VOLCANO** and is monitored closely for changes.

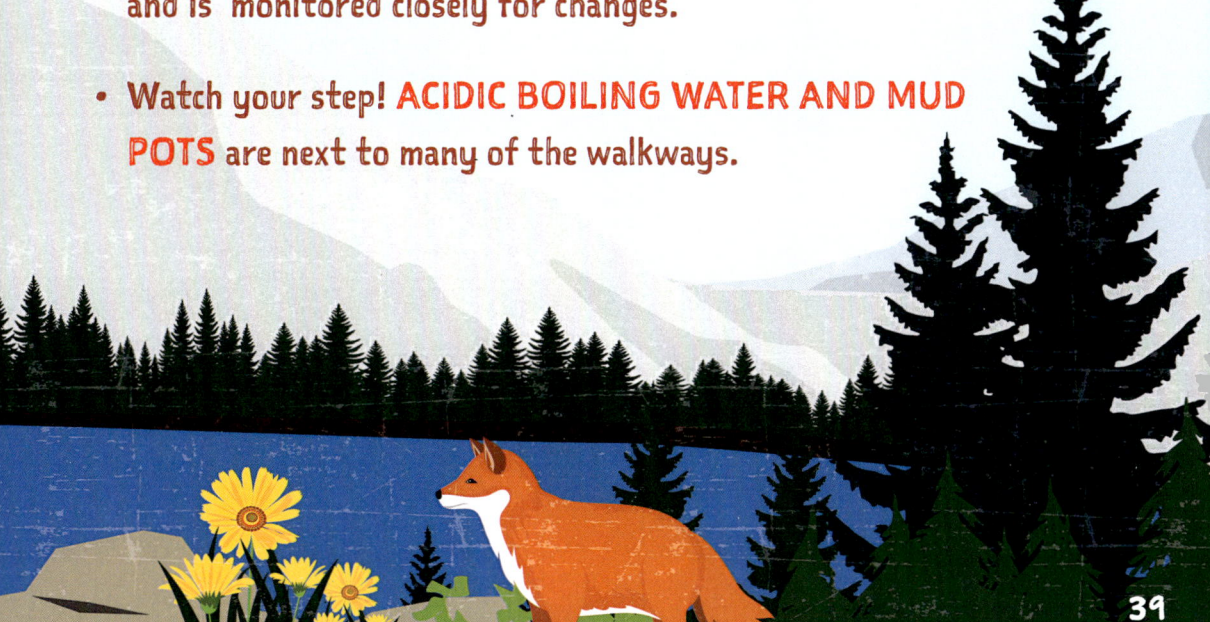

- Watch your step! **ACIDIC BOILING WATER AND MUD POTS** are next to many of the walkways.

PINNACLES NATIONAL PARK
California

26,686 acre park

59th National Park

Established in **2013**

42 square miles

Known for **Dramatic Rock Faces**

CA

40

PINNACLES NATIONAL PARK
Record Your Visit

Date: _____

This is the ____ park I've visited. We were in the park for _____ .
      #   hours/days

The weather was _____ .

My favorite memory of our visit was _____ .

I met Park Ranger _____ who has been here for _____ .
                                                                                             months/years

Their favorite part of the park is _____

_____ .

Park Ranger autograph:_____

Cancellation & Regional Stamp(s)

PINNACLES NATIONAL PARK
What to Look For

- There are roughly **400 SPECIES OF BEES** at Pinnacles.

- The **THREE-SPINED STICKLEBACK**, the only native fish here, can live in both fresh and salt water.

- **CHAPARRAL**, known by its tangled shrubs and thorny bushes, can be found just about everywhere you look.

- The **ROCK FORMATIONS** at Pinnacles are breathtaking and beautiful.

PINNACLES NATIONAL PARK
Interesting Facts

- **PINNACLES** has more than 30 miles of hiking trails.

- The ancient **CHALON AND MUTSUN TRIBES** foraged in Pinnacles for acorns as their primary food source.

- **RABBITS** were hunted for food by ancient peoples and their skins were cut into strips and woven into blankets and capes.

- **TALUS CAVES** are steep narrow canyons filled with boulders from the cliffs above.

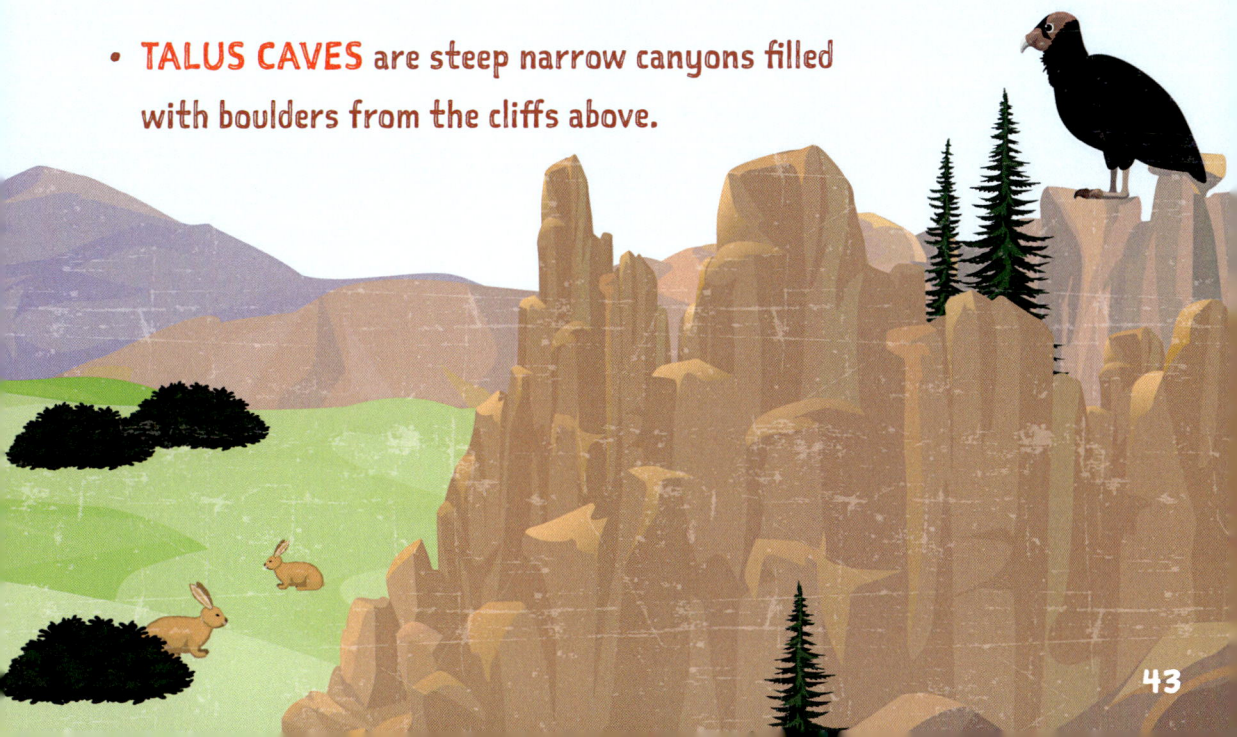

REDWOOD NATIONAL PARK
California

138,999 acre park

33rd National Park

Established in **1968**

217 square miles

The **Tallest Trees** on Earth

CA

11

44

REDWOOD NATIONAL PARK
Record Your Visit

Date: _____

This is the ____ park I've visited. We were in the park for _____ .
         #   hours/days

The weather was _____ .

My favorite memory of our visit was _____ .

I met Park Ranger _____ who has been here for _____ .
                                                                                                                    months/years

Their favorite part of the park is _____

_____ .

Park Ranger autograph: _____

Cancellation & Regional Stamp(s)

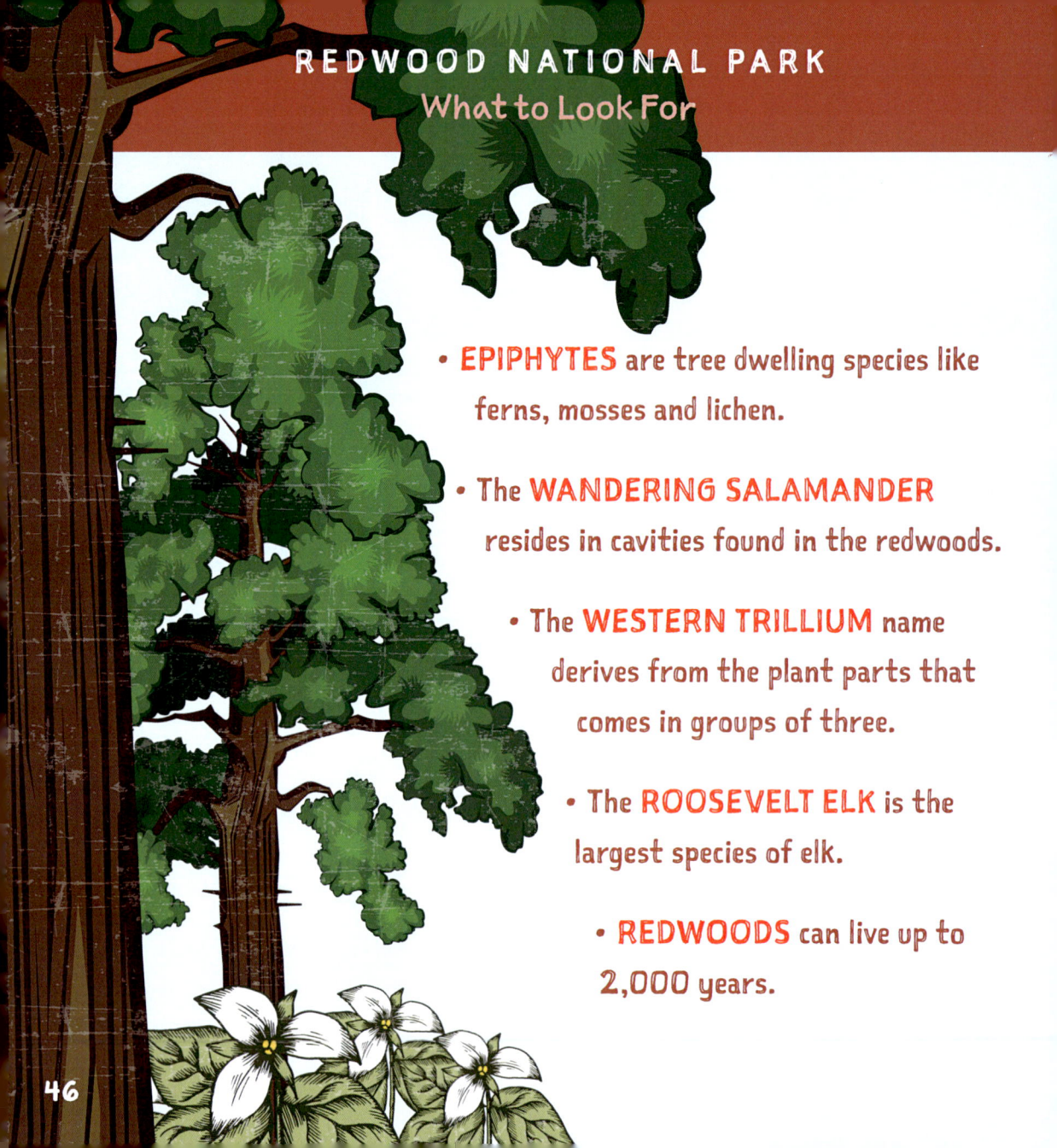

REDWOOD NATIONAL PARK
What to Look For

- **EPIPHYTES** are tree dwelling species like ferns, mosses and lichen.

- The **WANDERING SALAMANDER** resides in cavities found in the redwoods.

- The **WESTERN TRILLIUM** name derives from the plant parts that comes in groups of three.

- The **ROOSEVELT ELK** is the largest species of elk.

- **REDWOODS** can live up to 2,000 years.

REDWOOD NATIONAL PARK
Interesting Facts

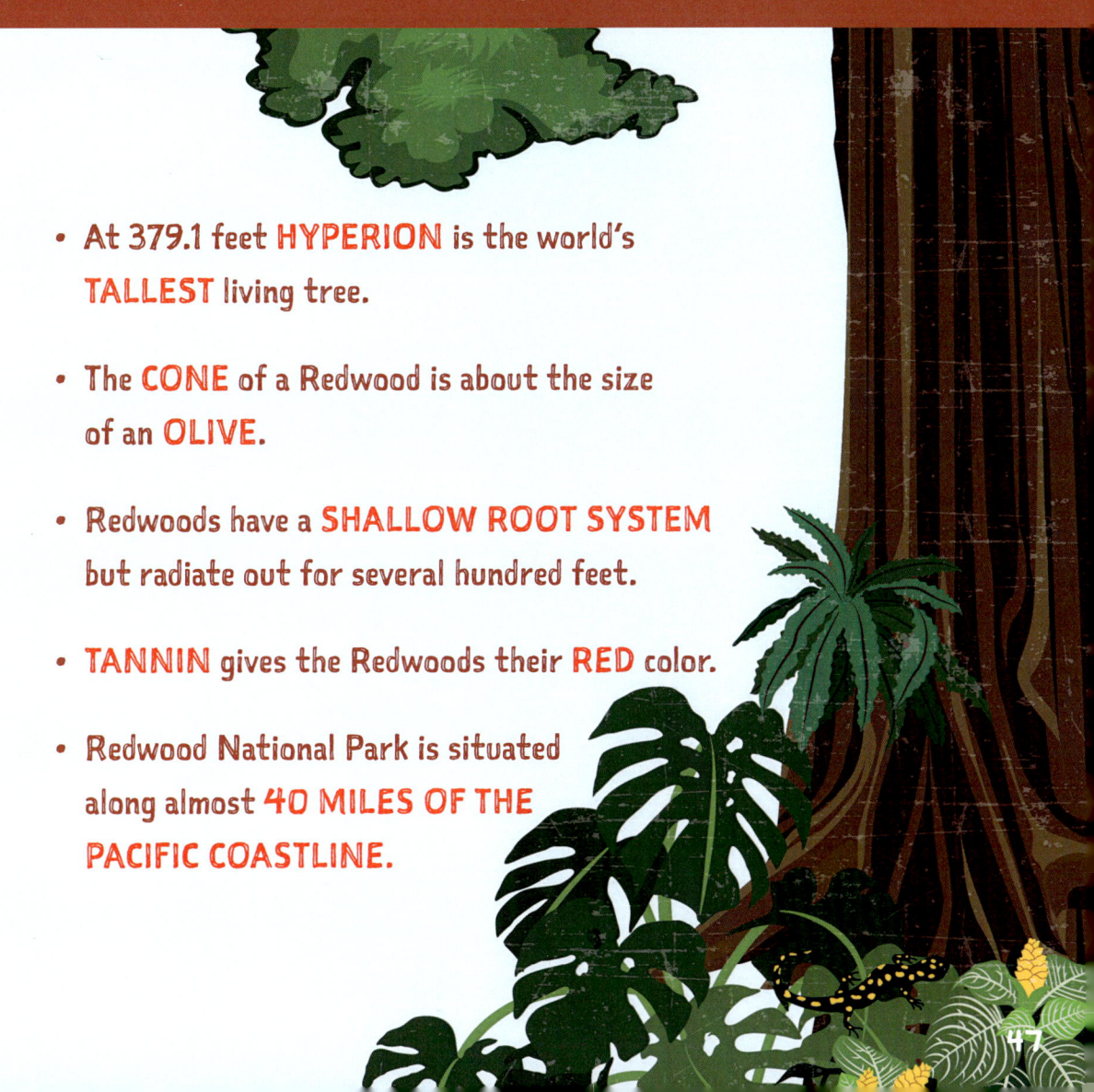

- At 379.1 feet **HYPERION** is the world's **TALLEST** living tree.

- The **CONE** of a Redwood is about the size of an **OLIVE**.

- Redwoods have a **SHALLOW ROOT SYSTEM** but radiate out for several hundred feet.

- **TANNIN** gives the Redwoods their **RED** color.

- Redwood National Park is situated along almost **40 MILES OF THE PACIFIC COASTLINE.**

SEQUOIA NATIONAL PARK
California

404,063 acre park

2nd National Park

Established in **1890**

631 square miles

General Sherman is the world's largest tree

CA
12

SEQUOIA NATIONAL PARK
Record Your Visit

Date: _____

This is the ____ park I've visited. We were in the park for _____ .
         #   hours/days

The weather was _____ .

My favorite memory of our visit was _____ .

I met Park Ranger _____ who has been here for _____ .
                                                                                          months/years

Their favorite part of the park is _____

_____ .

Park Ranger autograph: _____

Cancellation & Regional Stamp(s)

SEQUOIA NATIONAL PARK
What to Look For

- The **AMERICAN BLACK BEAR** ranges in color from cinnamon brown to black, and some have light blazes on their chests.

- Try to spot the **SMOKEY MARIPOSA LILY** by its three petals and yellow and dark red or black middle.

- The **GRAY-CROWNED ROSY FINCH**, a chunky, brownish finch with pink highlights and a gray crown, can be spotted flying.

- **SEQUOIAS** sprout from seeds. 91,000 sequoia seeds weigh just 1 pound.

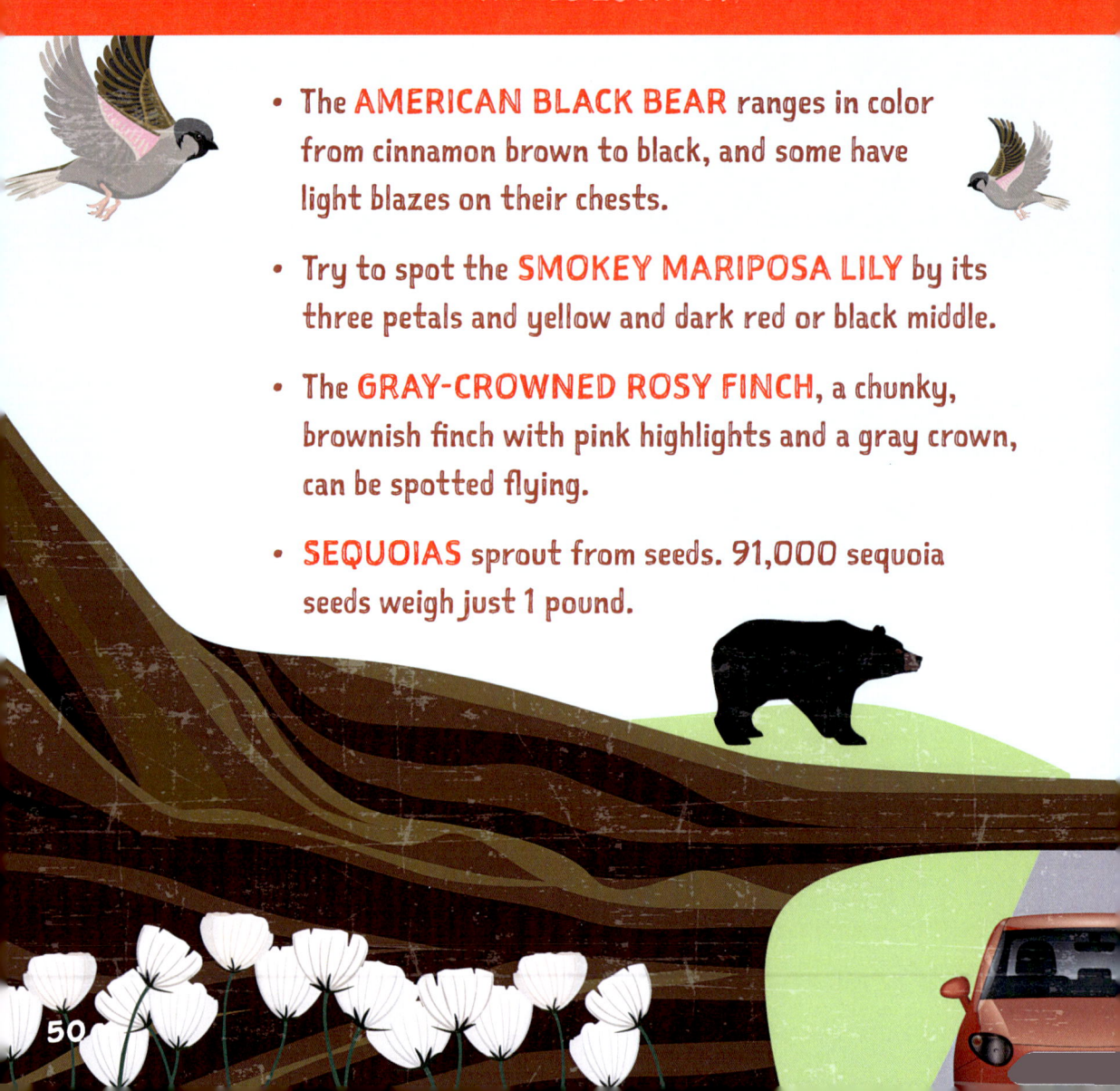

SEQUOIA NATIONAL PARK
Interesting Facts

- It is over 350 steps to the top of **MORO ROCK** which gives you spectacular views of the meadows, valleys, and other rock formations.

- Enjoy a ride through **"TUNNEL LOG."** This tree fell in 1937 and is used today as a tunnel through the park.

- In 1903 **COLONEL CHARLES YOUNG** was the first African American to be superintendent of a National Park.

- **CRYSTAL CAVE** is a marble cavern that can only be seen on guided tours.

YOSEMITE NATIONAL PARK
California

761,748 acre park

Established in **1890**

3rd National Park

282 miles of scenic roadways

CA

1,190 square miles

Yosemite is a **Glaciated Landscape**

YOSEMITE NATIONAL PARK
Record Your Visit

Date: _____

This is the ____ park I've visited. We were in the park for _____ .
     #   hours/days

The weather was _____ .

My favorite memory of our visit was _____ .

I met Park Ranger _____ who has been here for _____ .
                                                                                                 months/years

Their favorite part of the park is _____

_____ .

Park Ranger autograph:_____

Cancellation & Regional Stamp(s)

YOSEMITE NATIONAL PARK
What to Look For

- As a result of **GLACIATION**, landforms include jagged peaks, rounded domes, and u-shaped canyons.

- **PACIFIC FISHERS** are small, carnivorous mammals that look similar to a weasel.

- The **FOOTHILL-WOODLAND ZONE** is hot and dry in the summer with little or no snow in the winter. Plants include chamise, oak, and pine.

- The vibrant feathers of the **WESTERN TANAGERS** grace Yosemite's coniferous forests in summer.

YOSEMITE NATIONAL PARK
Interesting Facts

- Yosemite is located in the **SIERRA NEVADA MOUNTAINS**.

- **EL CAPITAN** and **HALF DOME** are two of the more famous rock formations in Yosemite.

- **JOHN MUIR WAS A NATURALIST** who wrote about the beauty of Yosemite.

- **ANSEL ADAMS WAS A PHOTOGRAPHER** whose art was inspired by Yosemite.

- Yosemite is home to many Waterfalls. **BRIDALVEIL FALLS** is often the first one visitors to the park see.

HALEAKALA NATIONAL PARK
Hawaii

28th National Park

52 square miles

33,265 acre park

Established in **1960**

Native Hawaiians cared for the land for over 1000 years

HALEAKALA NATIONAL PARK
Record Your Visit

Date: _____

This is the ____ park I've visited. We were in the park for _____ .
      #   hours/days

The weather was _____ .

My favorite memory of our visit was _____ .

I met Park Ranger _____ who has been here for _____ .
                                                                                                               months/years

Their favorite part of the park is _____

_____ .

Park Ranger autograph: _____

Cancellation & Regional Stamp(s)

HALEAKALA NATIONAL PARK
What to Look For

- The luminous **HALEAKALA SILVERSWORD** can live up to 90 years and only flowers once.

- Adult **`I`WI** are red, with striking black wings and an unmistakable slender, long, orange-colored bill.

- **NÉNÉ** are geese with distinctive "stripey" furrows on their white necks. If encountered on the ground, they produce the low "nay-nay" sound that they are named for.

- Over **850 SPECIES** of plants are found in this National Park.

HALEAKALA NATIONAL PARK
Interesting Facts

- **HALEAKALA** is on the Hawaiian Island of **MAUI**.

- The **SUMMIT** of Haleakala is **10,023 FEET**.

- The summit was called **WAO AKUA** by Native Hawaiians, meaning **WILDERNESS OF THE GODS**.

- Pools and Waterfalls can be found in the **KIPAHULA** District of Haleakala.

- **SUNRISE AND SUNSET VIEWING** on the summit is a popular activity.

HAWAI'I VOLCANOES NATIONAL PARK
Hawaii

29th National Park

323,431 acre park

Established in **1961**

Home to the largest **dragonfly** in the U.S.

HI 15

505 square miles

Provides refuge for **54** threatened and endangered species

HAWAI'I VOLCANOES NATIONAL PARK
Record Your Visit

Date: _____

This is the _____ park I've visited. We were in the park for _____ .
         #   hours/days

The weather was _____ .

My favorite memory of our visit was _____ .

I met Park Ranger _____ who has been here for _____ .
                                                                                                months/years

Their favorite part of the park is _____

_____ .

Park Ranger autograph: _____

Cancellation & Regional Stamp(s)

HAWAI'I VOLCANOES NATIONAL PARK
What to Look For

- The **HAWAIIAN HAWKSBILL TURTLE** or Honu'ea is protected on three beaches.

- The **'UA'U** seabird makes a call that sounds just like its name: oo-AH-oo.

- The **'OHI'A LEHUA** is a common tree in Hawai'i and its red Lehua flower is the official flower of the Big Island.

HAWAI'I VOLCANOES NATIONAL PARK
Interesting Facts

- The Hawaiian culture had a system of laws know as **KANAWAI** that enforced social order.

- **CAPTAIN JAMES COOK** arrived on the Hawaiian Islands in **1778**; his arrival disrupted the Hawaiian way of life.

- **PU'ULOA** has thousands of **PETROGLYPH ROCK CARVINGS** that can be seen as you walk along a boardwalk.

- **MAUNA LOA**, one of the world's most active volcanoes, rises from sea level to **13,677 feet**.

GREAT BASIN NATIONAL PARK
Nevada

Established in **1986**

49th National Park

NV

120 square miles

77,180 acre park

Bristlecone Pines have been known to live for 4,900 years

GREAT BASIN NATIONAL PARK
Record Your Visit

Date: _____

This is the ___ park I've visited. We were in the park for _____ .
       #   hours/days

The weather was _____ .

My favorite memory of our visit was _____ .

I met Park Ranger _____ who has been here for _____ .
                                                                                                                          months/years

Their favorite part of the park is _____

_____ .

Park Ranger autograph:_____

Cancellation & Regional Stamp(s)

GREAT BASIN NATIONAL PARK
What to Look For

- **BRISTLECONE PINES** are common in the park and survive the harshest of growing conditions.

- **KANGAROO RATS** live in underground tunnels throughout the park. They are amazing rodents able to live their entire lives without ever directly drinking water.

- Named for the spiky blossoms that resemble paintbrushes, the **INDIAN PAINTBRUSH** flower brings color to the sagebrush habitat.

- The **GREAT BASIN CAVE MILLIPEDE** is an endemic animal, meaning this is the only place on earth it is found.

GREAT BASIN NATIONAL PARK
Interesting Facts

- The **ANCIENT SHOSHONE** were hunters and gatherers and lived in temporary shelters know as **WIKIUPS**.

- In the 1880's **ABSALON LEHMAN** discovered a marble and limestone **CAVE** which has been named after him.

- **WHEELER PEAK SCENIC DRIVE** is a 12 mile adventure up more than 10,000 feet.

ALL NATIONAL PARKS

PACIFIC NORTHWEST & ALASKAN REGION
Alaska: Denali; Gates Of The Arctic; Glacier Bay; Katmai; Kenai Fjords; Kobuk Valley; Lake Clark; Wrangell-St. Elias
Oregon: Crater Lake
Washington: Mount Rainier; North Cascades; Olympic

WESTERN REGION
American Samoa: American Samoa
Arizona: Grand Canyon; Petrified Forest; Saguaro
California: Channel Islands; Death Valley; Joshua Tree; Kings Canyon; Lassen Volcanic; Pinnacles; Redwood; Sequoia; Yosemite
Hawaii: Haleakala; Hawai'i Volcanoes
Nevada: Great Basin

ROCKY MOUNTAIN REGION
Colorado: Black Canyon; Great Sand Dunes; Mesa Verde; Rocky Mountain
Montana: Glacier
North Dakota: Theodore Roosevelt
South Dakota: Badlands; Wind Cave
Utah: Arches; Bryce Canyon; Canyonlands; Capitol Reef; Zion
Wyoming: Grand Teton; Yellowstone

MIDWEST & CENTRAL REGION
Arkansas: Hot Springs
Indiana: Indiana Dunes
Michigan: Isle Royale
Minnesota: Voyageurs
Missouri: Gateway Arch
New Mexico: Carlsbad Caverns; White Sands
Ohio: Cuyahoga Valley
Texas: Big Bend; Guadalupe Mountains

EASTERN REGION
Florida: Biscayne; Dry Tortugas; Everglades
Kentucky: Mammoth Cave
Maine: Acadia
South Carolina: Congaree
Tennessee: Great Smoky Mountains
Virginia: Shenandoah
West Virginia: New River Gorge
USVI: U.S. Virgin Islands

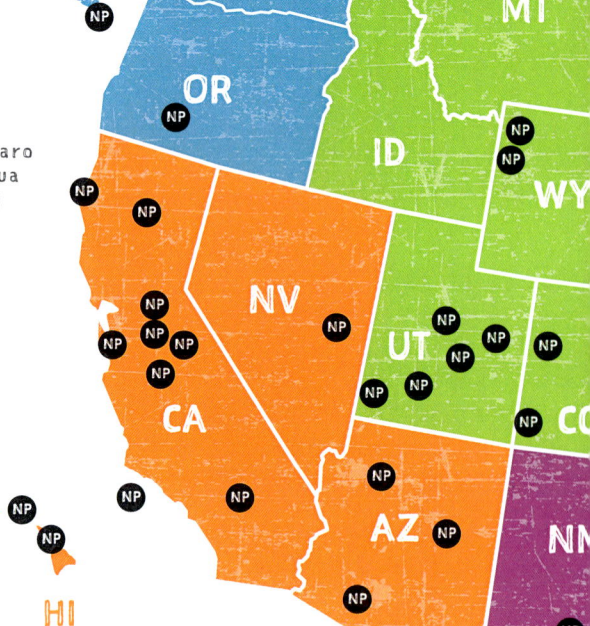